'But Who Do You Say That I Am?'

Quakers and Christ Today

Douglas Gwyn

Pendle Hill Pamphlet 426

About the Author

Douglas Gwyn grew up in the pastoral stream of Friends in Indiana. After experiencing a call to ministry in 1968, he attended Union Theological Seminary in New York City, where he began to know unprogrammed Friends better. Over the years, he has followed his calling to ministry into work as a Friends pastor, as a writer for the American Friends Service Committee, and as a teacher at the Quaker study centers Pendle Hill and Woodbrooke. His training in biblical studies has informed his research and writing on early Friends and on current issues among Friends today. Doug has coined the term "bispiritual" to describe Friends like himself who are engaged and nurtured by both pastoral and unprogrammed Friends, in different ways. His wife, Caroline Jones, is a Friend and dharma teacher in the Insight Buddhist tradition. Doug currently serves as Quaker Studies Teacher at Pendle Hill.

His books include *Apocalypse of the Word: The Life and Message of George Fox* (1986), *The Covenant Crucified: Quakers and the Rise of Capitalism* (1995), *Seekers Found: Atonement in Early Quaker Experience* (2000), and *Conversation with Christ: Quaker Meditations on the Gospel of John* (2011). He is currently completing two books, a history of Pendle Hill and a study of Quaker faith and practice as they contribute to a sustainable life.

Publications staff: Shirley Dodson

Pamphlet edited by Chel Avery and designed by Mary Helgesen Gabel

Requests for permission to quote should be addressed to:

Pendle Hill Publications, 338 Plush Mill Road, Wallingford, PA 19086-6023

Email: publications@pendlehill.org
ISBN 978-0-87574-426-1

February 2014

'But Who Do You Say That I Am?'

Quakers and Christ Today

One hears many different perspectives on Christ among Friends today. Some maintain the traditional Quaker-Christian faith. They identify the Light within as the presence of Christ in each person. They affirm this Christ within to be in some way one with the historical person of Jesus of Nazareth. At the other end of the spectrum are nontheist Friends, who reject not only the divinity of Christ but divinity in general. God is an old idea we have outgrown, or a word cluttered with too many meanings Friends do not embrace. Jesus was an ancient Jewish wisdom teacher who may have something to tell us moderns, but only as one among many sources, ancient and modern.

The majority of Friends in unprogrammed meetings today probably occupy a variety of positions between these two perspectives. Many are uncertain what they believe about Christ. They may voice one perspective in one situation and a different perspective in another.

Most strikingly, perhaps, these different perspectives on Christ are increasingly muted in the meeting for worship and in conversation among Friends. Christian Friends suppress their witness out of deference to others who may find their language offensive and excluding. Universalist and nontheist Friends likewise soft pedal their criticisms of Christianity in deference to Christian Friends. It is not uncommon for Christian Friends to assume that they are the only one left in their meeting, because they hear no one else speak of Christ. In contrast to the nineteenth-century painting of *The Presence in the Midst* in a Quaker meeting for worship, Christ has become something more like "the elephant in the living room" we hesitate to acknowledge.

While many Christian Friends (including myself some days) bemoan this situation, it is potentially a creative moment. In the Gospel of Mark, Jesus asks his disciples, "Who do people say that I am?" They respond that they have heard various ideas: a prophet, John the Baptist returned from the dead, and more. (They politely omit the negative views of Jesus also circulating—dangerous blasphemer, demon-possessed false prophet, libertine Sabbath breaker. But Jesus has confronted those himself.) Jesus then challenges them, "But who do you say that I am?" Only then does Simon Peter take the leap of faith and blurt out: "You are the Messiah." Surprisingly, at this pivotal moment, Jesus sternly orders them to tell no one about him (Mark 8:27-30).[1] Perhaps he understands that his power to heal people and change lives is greater in ambiguity than in certainty. He then goes on to describe what it means to be the Messiah—rejection and death. Peter's scandalized reaction reveals that even "the right answer" about Jesus raises profound and troubling new questions.

Today, after centuries of Christendom's affirmations that "Jesus is the answer," he is free at last to be the *question* again. After centuries in which Christian adherence served as a conformist cloak of social respectability for many, whatever their misgivings, confusions, and hypocrisies, the unabashed Christian is now rather suspect in growing sectors of western society. Now it is getting interesting! After centuries in the gilded cage of officially sanctioned religion, Jesus is free to be subversive again.

In this essay, I will examine and challenge the current range of perspectives on Christ among Quakers today. But first it seems appropriate to say something about my own journey and the viewpoint from which this essay is written.

My Own Testimony

I hope that this essay demonstrates more than theological training, historical study, or a personal preference for Christian faith. I write with a conviction grounded in life-changing experiences and forty years of Christian devotion and ministry. My Christian-universalist vision arises in part from key orienting experiences in early adulthood.

I grew up in a comfortable but not very challenging pastoral Friends meeting in the American Midwest. I received some basic Christian education while enjoying a warm and accepting religious environment that gave me nothing to rebel against but not much to kindle my spirit either. In my own experiences and inclinations, I was probably more of a nature-mystic than anything else.

At university I was a zoology major and starting to drift away from active involvement with any meeting or church when, in 1968, I received a distinct experience of calling to ministry. Alone one evening in my room, I perceived the words, "Be a minister." I had never for a moment considered that vocation. I was planning to become a scientist. Yet as I considered it, I began to realize that ministry named some gifts I might have and called me to grow into them. But I was not yet a Christian in any serious sense when I was called to be a minister.

Having grown up in a pastoral meeting, I understood ministry in the idiom of the pastor. So, after completing my first degree in zoology, I went on to train for ministry at Union Theological Seminary in New York. I discovered that I had good insights in interpreting the Bible. Perhaps owing in part to my science background, I was very interested in historical critical methods. (Union had been a stronghold of "higher criticism" even in the nineteenth century.) But critical re-readings of the Bible did not demolish its meaning for me—they added historical dimension and human texture.

As my personal growth progressed in relation to my theological training, I encountered Christ seriously for the first time. A second key orienting experience of my life occurred in meeting for worship at the Fifteenth Street Friends Meeting in New York in 1974. In the Spirit, I embraced the risen Christ and understood that everything he had done and had suffered was in love for me. That existential confrontation consolidated my being, gave me the sense of identity and confidence to "*be* a minister" and not just emulate others. It gave me the conviction to follow the call wherever it led, which has included periods of pastoral ministry among Friends, but has also involved the ministry of scholarship and writing, travel in ministry, and teaching at the Pendle Hill and Woodbrooke Quaker study centers.

Significantly, both of these key orienting experiences occurred at moments of crisis in my young life. God meets us at our extremity, where we are beyond our limits, when we despair of ourselves. Only then can God get past our defenses of competence and self-worth.

So my faith odyssey began somewhat like Abraham's, with the call of a God I did not know distinctly. That initiating experience has kept me open to the experience and understanding of people of other religious convictions, or of none. I would be untrue to my own experience if I were not. Yet at the same time, given my encounter with Christ, it would be disingenuous of me to stifle my Christian identity and understanding for the sake of fitting in with others.

These experiences undergird my answer to Jesus's query, "But who do you say that I am?" There is something absolutely unique in the person of Jesus of Nazareth, a crystalline expression of the love, wisdom, and will of God for all creation. Yet he is also universally human, as common as a carpenter's son from Galilee. His divinity and his humanity are one, inseparable—and so are ours. When we confess Jesus to be the Messiah, the hope of the world, we become part of that hope. We begin living into the gospel story as our story. Every answer about Jesus becomes over time an answer about ourselves.

A third key orienting experience early in my ministry is worth mentioning here. After a couple years of pastoral ministry back in Indiana, I returned to New York for doctoral studies in 1977. I had begun reading George Fox and was struck by his highly experiential way of interpreting the Bible, even the Book of Revelation. In my efforts to understand Fox and early Friends, I connected with Lewis Benson, who had studied and indexed Fox's writings more thoroughly than anyone. I learned a great deal from this high school dropout whose singular path of independent scholarship had evaded the usual frames of academic understanding. We did not agree on everything, but Lewis was a key mentor to me as I began my own journey of independent scholarship.

In learning from Fox and early Friends, I discovered a theological tradition that answered the Christian-universalist paradox of my own experience. Early and traditional Quaker Christian faith holds to both the biblical Christian *meaning* of the Light within and the universal *extent* of it in human experience. It has been one central concern of my ministry over the years to help Friends understand this paradox and to resist opting for one side or the other of its bewildering truth.

The Testimony of Early Friends

A free and mysterious Christ has been at the center of Quaker faith and practice from the beginning. George Fox's grand theme that "Christ is come to teach his people himself, and bring them off the world's ways and religions" was scandalous in seventeenth-century Puritan England. This Christ came not by way of an enfranchised clergy inculcating religious doctrine. This Christ came as promised, "like a thief" (Rev. 3:3), stealing into the world through each person's conscience, teaching men and women at a level below both Christian doctrine and human reason. Fox's Christ was the "subconscious" before Freud.

George Fox was thus neither the last great figure of the Protestant Reformation that had come before nor the vanguard of the liberal Enlightenment that would soon follow. He confronted men and women with an existential crisis. In the Christian-saturated culture of his day, he restated Jesus's question, "But who do you say that I am?" For example, he challenged a parish congregation at Ulverston in 1652: "You will say, Christ saith this, and the apostles say this, but what canst thou say? Art thou a child of the light, and hast thou walked in the light, and what thou speakest, is it inwardly from God?" To speak authentically of Christ is to become as a child, learning to walk all over again as the Light leads, learning to speak all over again from what truth the Light reveals.

Margaret Fell was there that day and was stricken, convicted by Fox's words. Sitting down in her pew, she wept bitterly, saying "We are all thieves, we are all thieves; we have taken the Scriptures in words and know nothing of them in ourselves."[2] Out of that painful but liberating moment of clarity, Fell quickly became Fox's great counterpart in building the Quaker movement.

But in the nineteenth century the Quaker conversation in Christ began to break down. Friends in both Britain and America were drawn into conversation with other vital streams in their culture. Some engaged with evangelical Christians and began to remodel their faith and practice according to evangelical Protestantism. Others engaged with Unitarians and other humanists and remodeled their faith and practice in that direction. In the United States, as Friends spread out over much larger geographical distances, these conversational drifts, accentuated by outright schisms, led to more drastic revisions of Quaker faith and practice than occurred in Britain.

In other words, on both sides of the Atlantic, Friends merged their Quaker-Christian understandings with either the Protestant Reformation or the liberal Enlightenment, the two great watersheds of modern Anglo-American culture. The uniquely Quaker understanding of Christ made less and less sense to Friends as they advanced further and further into these diverging conversations. In effect, we began responding to Jesus's first question, "Who do people say that I am?" That is, we took our cues from traditions other than our own. Those traditions have their own vitality and integrity, to be sure. But we lost something rare and precious when we stopped speaking in the Quaker voice, when we no longer knew how to make that voice our own and answer Jesus's second question, "But who do you say that I am?"

The challenge for Friends today is to encounter Christ neither from the viewpoint of a rapidly declining Christendom nor from the viewpoint of a rapidly advancing secular culture. It is to witness as the apostle Paul did in the first decades of the Christian movement:

From now on, therefore, we regard no one from a human point of view; even though we once knew Christ from a human point of view, we know him no longer in that way. So if anyone is in Christ, there is a new creation: everything old has passed away; see, everything has become new! All this is from God, who reconciled us to himself through Christ, and has given us the ministry of reconciliation [2 Cor. 5:16–18].

Thus, to be "in Christ," to become "a child of the Light," is a profound reorientation of viewpoint and motive. One passes beyond the confused human conversation *about* Christ and begins to live in conversation *with* Christ. And in that conversation, one's view not just of Christ but of everyone changes. The jostle of competition, condescension, and mistrust among human positions passes away and a compassionate, reconciling spirit takes its place. We find ourselves together in nothing less than a new creative process, in a divine wisdom beyond all reckoning.

This was the tremendously liberating message and energizing experience in the early Christian movement. The movement spread rapidly through the Roman Empire as a network of men and women who experienced Christ less as a "personal savior" (the framing of Christ in our modern, individualistic culture) than as a new *collective* reality. Christ was a new, multicultural, international personality in whom all could participate and interconnect. As such, the Christian movement was the first universalist faith. It posed a crucified Jewish Messiah as the subversive inversion of the violent dominion of Caesar's power. The sign of the cross served as a perpetual reproach to Rome and any power that represses the free movement of the Spirit among all the peoples of the earth. From that perspective, Christ as "Lord" and "King" was proclaimed only in the most ironic, deconstructive sense.

Only as Christ became "Christ" through the creedal formulations of later Church councils did this profoundly humanistic faith become a reified "religion" that alienated men and women from the presence and power of God among them. And as "Christianity" became the sanctioned and imposed ideology of Empire, "Jesus is Lord" lost its crucial, ironic sense. "Christ" became *mythic*, an explanation and justification for why the world is and must be as it is: violent, unjust, exploitative, unloving. The "kingdom of heaven," which Jesus proclaimed through parables as a wryly ironic and subtle reality, became the "pie in the sky" of another world after this one. It is revealing that the vestments still worn by cardinals today approximate the finery of the Roman aristocracy in the early centuries of the imperial Church.

But Christ's Spirit has not been so easily contained. As the Empire appropriated the Church, the desert fathers and mothers fled into the wilderness in order to revive and preserve the free Spirit of Christ. The peripheries of Christendom often maintained a high degree of autonomy in the first millennium. For example, Celtic Christianity was a creative synthesis of pagan and Christian beliefs and practices in western France, Britain, and Ireland. The pagan sense of the earth as a feminine, spiritual home melded with the more masculine energies of a collective human destiny in Christ. That synthesis was only slowly repressed by centralized Church authority over the course of centuries. It may well have been a subliminal influence in the rise of the early Quaker movement in northern England in the seventeenth century.

Let us now turn to the current range of Quaker perspectives on Christ and examine each from the reconciling perspective we heard witnessed by Paul. As in Paul's letters, this examination includes critical perspectives on each viewpoint (including my own). This overview is informed by a broad experience among Friends, including twelve years at Pendle Hill and four years at the

Woodbrooke Quaker Study Centre in England. I am also aided by conversation with my wife, Caroline Jones, who is a dharma teacher in the Insight Buddhist tradition. In addition, I have served at times as a Friends pastor in the American "programmed" branch of Friends. But I will limit this survey to the liberal "unprogrammed" branch, which will be the principle readership of this essay. I recognize that there are variations within every viewpoint characterized here. Some Friends may not feel accurately portrayed. But I hope this general mapping of the current Quaker landscape will serve a useful purpose.

Foundationist and Conservative Friends

Some Friends have rediscovered and embraced the unique Christian vision of early and traditional Quaker faith and practice. Typically, they have found it through reading historic Quaker writings or through contact with Conservative Friends in America. They find an understanding of Christ and a practice of Christian devotion that "speaks to their condition." That is, it answers their own actual experience and draws them into journeys of personal growth and courageous witness. Some are gay and lesbian Friends who left other Christian denominations where they were not welcomed. Others are Friends who were for many years satisfied with more humanist versions of Quaker faith and practice, but eventually found something more compelling in early Quaker writings.[3]

Friends in this stream generally fall into two categories (or some combination of the two). The first I will call *foundationist* Friends. They have been inspired by the radical, prophetic Christian witness of early Friends. Early Quaker writings are indeed remarkable for their integration of biblical language with personal experience. They are also socially radical. The Quaker testimonies we define today as peace, equality, community, simplicity, and integrity all find their beginnings in the early movement. For those inspired by early Friends, the foundational form of Quaker faith is normative. It is the measure by which all subsequent Quaker witness is tested—and usually found lacking.

Further, the resonances between the early Quaker and early Christian movements are compelling. Early Friends claimed to be "in the same spirit and power the prophets and apostles were in." William Penn called the Quaker movement "primitive Christianity revived." A return to the vitality of the early Church was a perennial dream of the Protestant Reformation. But while the Protestant Reformers had tried to renew early Christianity through chapter-and-verse reconstructions from the New Testament, early Friends immersed themselves in the power of the Spirit and let it re-invent the Church organically among them.

As a modern Friend and as an academically trained biblical interpreter, I personally take great inspiration from early Quaker witness. I have devoted many years to research and writing on early Friends in order to recover the integrity and power of their witness and to relate it to the struggles Friends face today. The most visible embodiment of the foundationist perspective among Friends is the New Foundation Fellowship, a group that formed in the 1970s around Lewis Benson and his systematic study of George Fox's writings.

The weakness of the foundationist perspective is the same one that neutralized the Protestant Reformation. Looking back over the Reformation, Fox wrote that it had left the Church in "heaps and confusion." That is, the Church (already long departed from a radical dependence upon the Spirit of Christ) had broken up into an assortment of state-church fiefdoms, each claiming to be the true Church, but whose very multiplicity belied them all. While foundationist Friends today do not generally identify Quaker faith and practice with Protestantism, they do have a tendency to assert that early Friends got it right, that theirs was the true Church. Therefore, the logic follows, if modern Friends would only return to early Quaker faith and practice, we would be the true Church again. That is the logic of Protestant sectarianism.

While there is much we can learn from early Friends (listening to them has deepened my own spiritual life and witness), we cannot simply repeat their words and expect them to have the same effect today. The early Christian and early Quaker movements were born of a sense of crisis, an *apocalyptic* sense that a world was ending and that a new world (Paul's "new creation") was beginning.

The early Christian movement began as a crisis in first-century Judaism, which was crumbling under the Roman occupation. Jesus catalyzed a grassroots revolutionary movement, a nonviolent alternative to both the collaborationist regime of the chief priests and the violent revolutionary aspirations of the Zealots. After Jesus was handed over to the Romans to be crucified as a political criminal, the situation in Palestine degenerated until a Zealot-led revolt brought the destruction of Jerusalem and the end of their temple-centered world. In the meantime, the Christian movement had metamorphosed into an international movement and spread to become a growing crisis in the Roman Empire. That crisis was experienced among all kinds of peoples within the Empire. They began to know themselves as a new, universal humanity in Christ, a subversion of the vast, oppressive power of Rome.

Sixteen hundred years later, for early Friends, the crisis was the outcome of the English Civil War, which had left a stalemate in both religion and politics. Friends were key actors in the end of a feudal world and the emergence of modernity. They quickly spread to become a trans-Atlantic community pioneering in religious freedom, peaceful approaches to conflict, and the growth of democratic society.

Any Christian renewal among Friends that draws upon the foundations of our faith and practice will be stillborn if it sits quietly in sectarian rectitude. It will prove regressive if it gets lost in its seventeenth-century frame of reference (my own personal *caveat*). The strengths of Quaker faith and practice must be brought to bear upon the sense of crisis that is unique to our own time.

So my query to foundationist Friends might be posed thus: *What is the crisis of our time? What world is ending? Who do you say Christ is in this situation? Where is the new creation unfolding?*

Conservative Friends share an interest in early Quaker witness, but are particularly drawn to the classical Quaker faith and practice of the eighteenth and early nineteenth centuries. They are inspired by the example of Conservative Friends in the United States. That small group of mostly rural Friends has retained more of traditional Quaker practices than have the larger evangelical or liberal Quaker streams.

Thus, while the new Conservative Friends are Christ-centered in their *faith*, they are often most drawn by the *practices* of traditional Friends. These include deeper meetings for worship, a more worshipful and disciplined business method, the recognized leadership of recorded (but still nonprofessional) ministers, the authority of elders to mentor Friends into a deeper spiritual life and a more courageous lived testimony, and the explicit answering of the Quaker queries, rather than using them simply as rhetorical questions.

Given their traditionalist orientation, many Friends in the Conservative renewal are surprisingly technophilic. For example, many pursue their concerns through blogs and other web-based media. The Friends of the Light group in Britain[4] holds online meetings for worship. But Conservative Quakers are also a countercultural phenomenon: Quaker process is seen as a corrective to the distracting consumerist tendencies of a media-saturated society.

In the final analysis, Quaker renewal will not come through refined technique. Traditional Quaker practices developed through a community's lived relationships in Christ. The example of Jesus as a servant-leader, together with the deep surrender required for us to stand steadfastly in the Light of Christ, provide us with the humble strength to bear one another's burdens and make the sacrifices required to function as a community in the long term. Without our participation in the transcendent personality of Christ, in whom differences are reconciled and sins forgiven, we are simply too self-interested, too brittle and short-sighted, to thrive together.

So my query to the new Conservative Friends might be as follows: *Who do you say Christ is? How do you find his personality revealed in good Quaker process? What is the heart that beats in the midst of a truly gathered meeting for worship? What is the mind that guides the meeting for business at its best?*[5]

Ecumenical and Interfaith Friends

The first generation of Friends believed they had been gathered by Christ into "heavenly Mount Sion," a spiritual place that transcended the stalemated religious controversies of the Reformation and the bloody political strife of the English Civil War. They saw themselves on the vanguard of God's redeeming work in history and believed that the rest of the world would soon follow them into this new intimacy with Christ and with one another. But sustained, violent persecution eventually forced them to abandon their revolutionary stance and adopt a more hedged, sectarian posture. In so doing, they were able to preserve their countercultural spirituality, ethics, and group processes for the long term.

As we have seen, the early Quaker prophetic mode and the traditional Quaker sectarian mode most inspire foundationist and Conservative Friends. Certainly, many other Friends today also cherish the unique Quaker approach that has nurtured their spiritual lives. But they also find spiritual riches in other traditions. Some are drawn into collaboration with other Christian churches, others into dialogue with non-Christian groups. These *ecumenical* and *interfaith* Friends are motivated by a variety of leadings and concerns that deserve our appreciative but critical attention.

Ecumenical Friends engage locally, nationally, and internationally in Christian dialogue and collaborative action with other churches. Friends have official membership in ecumenical organizations such as Churches Together in Britain and Ireland, the National Council of Churches in the United States, and the World Council of Churches. They also engage in a variety of local and regional collaborations with churches: food pantries, charity work, prison and hospital chaplaincies, peace and justice witness, environmental action, and more. Thus, Friends unite with other Christians most typically in devotion to the Lord who came in the form of a servant to all. For the sake of shared Christian faith and social concern, these Friends are willing to put aside historic Quaker criticisms of the Christian mainstream and recognize that our different churches today speak to (and for) different personality types and cultural preferences.

The conviction that the Light of Christ is in each person nurtures in Friends a high receptivity to human difference. Quaker faith engenders a spiritual hospitality that "makes room at the table" for all. But Friends are often inarticulate in witnessing their own faith to others. This reticence arises in part from the muting of Christian conversation in our meetings (noted near the beginning of this essay). We are not practiced in witnessing to Christ, even among ourselves, even when our faith is ardent.

But our reticence is also attributable to a historic Quaker preference for narrative theology over doctrinal formulations. Traditional Quaker literature is robustly Christian. But because our faith is rooted in individual and group *experience*, our classic literary expressions of faith have been spiritual autobiography and Quaker history. So even in dialogue with our closest spiritual cousins, the other historic peace churches (Mennonites and the Church of the Brethren), Friends can be surprisingly shy theologically. We prefer story telling over doctrinal propositions.

Occasionally, Friends are forced to define their faith more clearly for the sake of maintaining both ecumenical ties and theological distinctiveness. A notable example arose in the 1980s, when the World Council of Churches was engaged in defining membership in terms of baptism, eucharist, and ministry. Friends were forced either to opt out or make the case for their unique approach to all three. British Friends published *To Lima with Love* (1987), which contributed to the WCC's acceptance of the exceptional position of Friends.

My query to ecumenically engaged Friends might be posed as follows: *Who do you say that Christ is to your Christian sisters and brothers? How do you tell the story of your faith as you serve the poor and witness for peace and justice alongside more doctrinally and liturgically minded Christians?*

Interfaith Friends are often involved in ecumenical work as well. But the two concerns are not identical, and interfaith work often arises from a different complex of concerns. For some, particularly those engaging in dialogue with Jews and Muslims, the Quaker peace testimony is often a prime motivator. The Holocaust of World War II and the "War on Terror" after September 11, 2001, have mobilized Friends to seek avenues of understanding to prevent future violence. Our Quaker gift of spiritual hospitality invites others to speak in healing ways of their faith, their hurts, and their hopes. Friends engaged in these conversations often mute their Christian viewpoint, owing in part to the violence that mainstream Christianity has historically tolerated—or even advocated—against Jews and Muslims.

But Judaism and Islam are faiths with strong identities and particular convictions. Their adherents respect those qualities in other faiths. Muslims in particular are suspicious of western, secular relativism. True interfaith *dialogue* does not begin until Friends speak from the depths of their own tradition. Christianity, Islam, and Judaism—grounded in overlapping scriptures and history—are all strongly dialogical faiths. When we fail to keep up our side of the dialogue, we may be viewed as either confused or patronizing.

But contemporary Quaker reticence also arises in part from the decline in recorded ministry among Friends. The recording of ministers was the overt recognition by meetings that some men and women have a particular gift in prophetic or teaching ministry. The traditional Friends minister spoke spontaneously in meeting for worship but also studied and meditated upon scripture. His or her ministry carried on a dialogue between scripture and lived experience. A number of such ministers left "journals," autobiographies that describe their spiritual lives, their calling, development, and travels in ministry. Journals narrate how they found biblical stories and truths confirmed in their own lives. Quaker journals served as templates for spiritual formation among Friends. They maintained a living Christian understanding and witness among Friends.

For better and worse, the spread of university education among Friends added competing and proliferating templates for understanding the Quaker spiritual experience. The traditional spiritual authority of the humble Friends minister, who might not be formally educated at all, was gradually displaced by the articulate religious ideas of MAs and PhDs in the meeting. The resulting equivalence and exchange of religious ideas led over time to equivocation and the equal standing of all sincerely held views.

Hence, in our interfaith relations with Jews and Muslims, we often provide no partner in dialogue with the rabbi and the imam, with those who are steeped in their faith and mentored in their tradition. Jews and Muslims instead hear oblique remarks from a variety of Friends, each hesitating to speak for Friends generally. This can sometimes be interpreted as evasion.

A different subgroup of interfaith Friends typically engages in conversation with Hindus and Buddhists. Here a post-Christian perspective is often more explicit and there is a positive attraction to the very different frameworks of eastern thought and spirituality. In particular, many Friends today find energizing affinities between Buddhist and Quaker practices. In an era where technology and technique are strong cultural determinants, the more explicit guidance found in eastern meditation is especially attractive. By contrast, Friends have steadfastly resisted explicit definitions of what it means to "wait upon the Lord," "stand still in the Light," or "sink down to the Seed." These traditional metaphors were intended to draw one into the unique space created by biblical stories, the teachings of Jesus, and the transcendent personality of Christ. Where they are no longer understood or embraced, Friends may understandably find themselves at loose ends in Quaker worship and the "daily retirement of mind."

Moreover, Buddhist nontheism is particularly attractive to many post-Christian, universalist, or nontheist Friends. Some look to the East as a way out of the entire western mindset—Christian, theist, or secular. Here, engagement is often less a dialogue than a hybridization. There is a growing Quaker-Buddhist phenomenon, in which Friends meld the two spiritual traditions, combining what they find useful in each, ignoring the rest. Other "Quaker hyphens" include Quaker-pagan and Quaker-Wicca. Each seeks to link contemporary Quaker practice with traditions outside Christian, patriarchal, and techno-capitalist social structures. These avenues of exploration can be fruitful for Friends on an individual level. But they are often based on a limited acquaintance with Quaker faith and practice.

Hence, to my Friends engaging with Jews and Muslims: *Who do you say Christ is, to those who have suffered violence and exclusion by westerners who call themselves Christian? Who do you say Christ is in relation to the people who gave birth to and nurtured Jesus of Nazareth? Who do you say Christ is to the followers of Mohammed, who recognized Jesus as a great prophet and reached out to Jews and Christians, seeking unity?*

To Friends engaging with Buddhists and Hindus: *Who do you say Christ is, in contrast to the western heritage of economic and cultural imperialism that has appropriated Christ, along with the rest of us? Have you met this Christ? If so, what has this Christ to say to Krishna? To the Buddha?*

Universalist and Nontheist Friends

There has been a universalist dimension to Quaker-Christian faith from the beginning. It is grounded in a paradox that cannot be resolved, only lived. From the beginning, Friends affirmed that the Light in their consciences is the presence of the risen Christ. That is, this Light is one with the person of Jesus of Nazareth, whose Sermon on the Mount lays the groundwork for the Quaker social testimonies, whose preaching of the kingdom of heaven within and among us calls us to find truth, peace, and justice here in this life, whose death and resurrection invite us to die to self and live to God and to one another.

But paradoxically, this same Light is in all people, in all places and times. It shines in people who do not believe the gospel or who have never heard it preached. They too can turn to this Light, enter God's counsel, and live blessed, redeemed, enlightened lives without a Christian set of beliefs. This universalist aspect of the Quaker faith was scandalous to the Puritan contemporaries of early Friends. It still disturbs many other Christians to this day.

Hence, Friends are historic pioneers in a more inclusive Christian faith. But it is a paradox modern Friends have found difficult to hold together. We tend to embrace either the Christian *meaning* or the universal *extent* of the Light. In America, some evangelical Friends have gone so far as to deny the universal presence of the Light, because it makes Christian faith too ambiguous. Meanwhile, some liberal Friends in America and Britain wish to shed Christian faith as an atavism we moderns can leave behind, in order to embrace an unambiguous universalism. This trend grew over the course of the twentieth century. At the beginning of that century, liberal Quaker reformers such as Rufus Jones and John Wilhelm Rowntree sought to move Friends beyond the evangelical preoccupation with doctrines. They reframed "Quakerism" as a *mystical* religion, a religion of *experience.* While these leaders still wrote from a Christian viewpoint, the emphasis upon personal experience inevitably gained more humanistic and cross-cultural overtones as the century progressed and secularization advanced. And as more Friends encountered non-Christian religions in the postcolonial, multicultural world of the latter twentieth century, they sought a more cosmopolitan outlook to reframe their Quaker faith and practice.

By the 1970s, the Quaker Universalist Group in Britain and the Quaker Universalist Fellowship in America became focal points for the new post-Christian perspective. In the 1970s and 1980s, Quaker universalists engaged in critical dialogue with Christ-centered Friends. This was generally a useful conversation, though

Friends often talked past each other, and some yearly meetings experienced debilitating conflict over the issues.

By the beginning of this century, a *nontheist* voice emerged more clearly among universalist Friends. Nontheism names a viewpoint that was probably present among Quaker universalists all along. The growing Quaker-Buddhist interchange may have inspired nontheist Friends to state their position more clearly. Meanwhile, other social factors have contributed. Continuing secularization brackets "God" into smaller corners of our consciousness and more delimited social enclaves, away from public view and polite conversation. Meanwhile, the news media, with an eye toward entertainment value, tend to highlight conflict between caricatured protagonists. That tendency has promoted stereotypical images of Christians and Muslims as fundamentalists and political reactionaries. "God" becomes the bogeyman and a drag on social progress for many educated, liberal-minded cosmopolitans, including some Friends.

This trend is evidenced by some recent published writings by nontheist Friends. David Rush, an American Friend, helpfully published his survey of 199 nontheist Friends in Britain and America in 2002.[6] Rush quotes several statements revealing caricatured and prejudiced views of Christians among nontheist Friends who are clearly uninformed about the varieties of Christian faith today. The essay concludes by offering a humanistic argument on behalf of a nontheist Quakerism, suggesting that it is not Quaker practice to exclude anyone.

A similar outlook is evinced by David Boulton, a British Friend, in *The Trouble with God: Building the Republic of Heaven.*[7] His book is written for those who, in poet Stevie Smith's words, cannot "bear much longer the dishonesty/Of clinging for comfort to beliefs we do not believe in . . . will not allow good to be hitched to a lie" (p. xiv). Of course, I have already suggested that the world will be well rid of such hypocritical, fear-based belief. But Boulton seems not to know those for whom Christian faith is a courageous, compassionate, and socially progressive life. He addresses the journalistic stereotypes of Christian and Islamic fundamentalism that have come to represent theism generally.

Compare Boulton's outlook with Jonathan Dale's socially engaged writings, such as *Quaker Social Testimony in Our Personal and Corporate Life*.[8] Dale, another British Friend, has worked many years with a housing cooperative in Salford, England. He suggests that Friends have been "seduced by the dominant intellectual spirit of the age," by a secularism satisfied with "pursuing self-interest under skies swept clean not only of 'the old man with the beard' but all transcendence" (pp. 5–6). He advocates a renewal of shared social testimony and advocacy as the best defense against "liberal Quakerism's besetting sin of subjectivism" (p. 26). Dale does not write as a Christian, but he models and advocates the social transcendent life that forms the basis of a transcendent faith. This was the genius of the early Church, as witnessed by Paul, where "there is no longer Jew or Greek, there is no longer slave or free, there is no longer male and female; for all of you are one in Christ Jesus" (Gal. 3:28).

The Religious Society of Friends today, at least in its liberal stream, must beware of its middle-class, educated frame of reference. Without critical self-awareness, Friends risk becoming a liberal sect. In other words, we find ourselves speaking an idiomatically Quaker dialect of a vague, cosmopolitan Esperanto. The growth of a large middle-class sector is one of the great accomplishments of modern, liberal democracy. But the middle-class conformity that once made Christianity stink with hypocrisy can function just as powerfully under other guises.

From another perspective, some nontheist and other universalist Friends still hold to a modernist sense of progress, an ever-upward-and-onward human destiny. This view is often couched in a *scientistic* outlook. By this I mean science as an ideological worldview, rather than a rigorous method of investigating the world. Scientism often views Christianity and all premodern religions as superstitions to be cast off and outgrown. By contrast, science itself can complement religious faith, investigating *how* the world works, without needing to confirm *or* deny religious convictions regarding divine wisdom and purpose.

But if a scientistic outlook will not embrace Christ, it can still scrutinize Jesus. A number of post-Christian Friends have taken great interest in the work of the Jesus Seminar, an international group of New Testament scholars who apply critical methods to discover "the real Jesus" behind the ancient theological trappings of the gospel texts. The Seminar and its publisher have sought to present their work as a bold new enterprise, though the search for the historical Jesus goes back through the nineteenth century. A century ago, Albert Schweitzer wryly summarized the dilemma in *The Quest of the Historical Jesus* (1910): searching for the historical Jesus is like looking down a well. You see a face down there and peer intently to make out its features. Sooner or later, you realize the face to be your own. And surely enough, the Jesus Seminar peered intently, with the best critical methods, and decided that Jesus was not a healer or apocalyptic prophet but a teacher of wisdom (these men and women are of course academics).

By contrast, Schweitzer poses Jesus as someone far more enigmatic:

> Jesus as a concrete historical personality remains a stranger to our time, but His spirit, which lies hidden in His words, is known in simplicity, and its influence is direct. Every saying contains in its own way the whole Jesus. The very strangeness and unconditionedness in which He stands before us makes

it easier for individuals to find their own personal standpoint in regard to Him.

He comes to us as One unknown, without a name, as of old, by the lake-side, He came to those men who knew Him not. He speaks to us the same word: "Follow thou me!" and sets us to the tasks which He has to fulfill for our time. He commands. And to those who obey Him, whether they be wise or simple, He will reveal Himself in the toils, the conflicts, the sufferings which they shall pass through in His fellowship, and, as an ineffable mystery, they shall learn in their own experience Who He is.[9]

Thus, Schweitzer suggests that we know the real Jesus as we follow him into service. As we transcend ourselves and our social location through service, hospitality, and stewardship of our resources, we come to know the transcendent personality of Christ—and recognize that personality (risen or imprisoned) in each person we engage.

This Jesus is the Christ witnessed in an early hymn quoted by Paul in his letter to the Philippians (2:6-8):

Who, though he was in the form of God, did not regard equality with God as something to be exploited, but emptied himself, taking the form of a servant, being born in human likeness. And being found in human form, he humbled himself and became obedient to the point of death—even death on a cross.

Equality, the great touchstone of a middle-class worldview, makes for good civil society, but it does not by itself create the blessed community. Servanthood—pouring ourselves out into a form less dignified but more useful—puts us in the form of Christ in the world. Are we Friends prepared to be servants, or only equals?

So, to answer my nontheist Friends, yes, Nietzsche was right: God is dead. But that is a part of the Christian faith (one we Christians too rarely dare to contemplate). Christ did not take *part* of God but *all* of God into human form, even to death on a cross. And if his cry of abandonment had been his last word on the cross, it would have been the last word on God. But in then offering up his spirit into God's hands, Jesus brought heaven and earth together. His death was not an appeasement to an angry God glowering down from heaven at humans. It was the reconciliation of God and human in the reconciliation of human with human:

> For he is our peace; in his flesh he has made both groups [any combination of groups] into one and has broken down the dividing wall, that is, *the hostility between us* . . . that he might create in himself one new humanity in place of the two, thus making peace, and might reconcile both groups to God in one body through the cross, thus putting to death that hostility through it [Eph. 2:14-16, italics added].

The forgiveness Jesus preached from the beginning of his ministry reached its ultimate expression in the cross and is realized as we forgive one another and find common purpose in serving and freeing others. God re-emerges as Christ among us. But the death of God is a crucial moment in that process. Otherwise, theism lives up to its bad reputation as a projection upon the heavens of our own wishful thinking and old grudges.

As the late Walter Wink, the New Testament interpreter, suggested, the raising of Jesus from the dead is an objective fact of history, even if it was not empirically observable.[10] That is, he became a living presence to so many different kinds of human beings in the next few years, his new life is undeniable. Mercurial networks of the Christian movement spread as an irrepressible force throughout the Roman Empire. His life (or blood, in ancient sacrificial terminology) flowed from him on the cross into humanity at large. The cruel Roman execution of a political subversive became the subversion of the Empire in love and mutuality. His spirit was "poured out on all flesh," as the prophet Joel had prophesied and as Peter witnessed at Pentecost (Acts 2:17). His light enlightens every one who comes into the world as John testifies (1:9). For "through him God was pleased to reconcile to himself all things, whether on earth or in heaven, by making peace through the blood of his cross" (Col. 1:20).

None of this could be without the death of God. And as we witness the decline of Christendom in the West, the death of God has an entirely new currency. As I suggested at the start of this essay, this is a moment of great new possibility. Christ is free again to move at large in surprising and liberating ways. But only those who see past the world's wisdom will recognize his form and follow his movements. And those who follow will not be recognized by the world, for "your life is hidden with Christ in God" (Col. 3:3). It can just as well be said that God is hidden with Christ in your life. Hence, many will continue in their impressions that God is dead and that you are a fool. Yes, God is dead and we are fools, *but we see the irony in it, we feel the infinite joy in it, we know the immeasurable riches of fellowship with Christ and with one another in service.*

So, queries for universalist and nontheist Friends to consider might include these: *Who is the Christ you have outgrown or find incredible? Are you judging Christ according to caricatures of Christians (some of them real enough)? Have you really encountered this mysterious figure in the gospels? In your heart? Are you prepared to grapple with the deep paradoxes and troubling ironies of a mature Christian faith? You can report what others—believers and disbelievers—have said of Christ, but what canst thou say?*

May the conversation between Christian and nontheist Friends continue to mature. John Lampen strikes a fine balance:

> To apply the term "God" (in the Christian sense) is to say that we perceive intuitively a connection between the marvels of the natural world, the moral law, the life of Jesus, the depths of the human personality, our intimations about time, death and eternity, our experience of human forgiveness and love, and the finest insights of the Christian tradition. To deny the existence of "God" is to say that we cannot (yet) see such connections. But even the word "God" is not an essential tool for grasping them.[11]

The Banished Host

Jesus saw his mission to gather "the lost sheep of the house of Israel" (Matt. 15:24). His Sermon on the Mount preached a radical social ethic grounded in a living experience of *shalom*, the kingdom of heaven spreading among people. He invited back into the house of Israel Jewish peasants who could not keep the elaborate cultic regimens of the Scribes and Pharisees. Jesus reached out not only to the poor but to a variety of social and religious outcasts, including prostitutes and tax collectors. He was able to evoke in a wide variety of people a sense of divine presence and power to heal not only physical and mental illnesses, but the many forms of alienation separating them from God and from one another. Again, spiritual transcendence and social transcendence were intimately woven together in the movement Jesus catalyzed in the few short years of his recorded ministry.

But Jesus also interacted with a variety of individuals beyond the ethnic boundaries of his people. When he was boldly importuned by a Canaanite woman to heal her daughter, Jesus recognized the strength of her faith (Matt. 15:21-28). When traveling through Samaria, he had conversation with a woman whose insights engaged him at a high level (John 4:1-26). He was "amazed" at the faith of a Roman centurion, who asked him to heal his servant (Luke 7:1-10). These scattered contacts prefigure the wider mission of the movement that followed his death.

But Jesus was a faithful Jew who came "not to abolish but to fulfill" the law and prophets (Matt. 5:17). He had sympathizers, friends, and followers among the Scribes and Pharisees. If his ministry took him to the margins of his people and beyond, he was in no way inclined to forsake those at the center, even at the risk and eventual loss of his own life at the hands of those who found him a threat to their establishment.

The ethic of Jesus can thus be understood as one of *radical hospitality*. His parables constantly invite people into fellowship, sharing, and mutual forgiveness. There is room for everyone at the table (Luke 14:7-24). Ironically, however, Jesus had no home, no table prepared for guests. He lived by the kindness of strangers and interested listeners. Their hospitality to him created the space for him to open their hearts to others. For example, he invited himself to dinner in the home of Zacchaeus, a despised tax collector. Neighbors grumbled that he would be the guest of a notorious sinner. But for his part, Zacchaeus was so moved by this gesture of inclusion, he promised to make restitution to those whom he had cheated. Jesus responded to Zacchaeus before the crowd of neighbors: "Today salvation has come to this house, because he too is a son of Abraham. For the Son of Man came to seek out and to save the lost" (Luke 19:9–10). To multiply his ministry, Jesus trained a core group of seventy disciples in a life of itinerant preaching, instructing them to enter the doors that were opened to them (Luke 10:1-24).

The fatal conflict of Jesus's ministry took place at the temple in Jerusalem, the symbolic and economic center of Jewish society. Jesus confronted the money changers and the sellers of sacrificial animals: "Take these things out of here! Stop making my Father's house a marketplace!" (John 2:16). The central religious institution of the people had become an inhospitable place. Henceforth, the chief priests viewed Jesus as a dire threat to their power. Handing Jesus over to the Roman occupation broke the ancient desert code of hospitality, protection of the guest against enemies. David had sung to the Lord, "You prepare a table before me in the presence of my enemies, you anoint my head with oil; my cup overflows. Surely goodness and mercy shall follow me all the days of my life, and I shall dwell in the house of the Lord my whole life long" (Ps. 23:5–6). There was no temple in Jerusalem when David sang that song. "The house of the Lord" was an indeterminate space of mutual hospitality in the Spirit of the Lord.

The international Christian movement that followed Jesus's death replicated and expanded his ethic of hospitality in a variety of ways. The writer of 1 Peter describes the movement as a "spiritual house" made of "living stones" around Christ the cornerstone. They are a "royal priesthood" that offers "spiritual sacrifices" in the acts of mutual aid, in hospitality to strangers, and in their vocation to "proclaim the mighty acts of him who called you out of darkness into his marvelous light. Once you were not a people, but now you are God's people; once you had not received mercy, but now you have received mercy" (2:9–10). In being merciful to strangers they were no longer strangers to the God they now experienced in their midst.

Yet ironically, they were now "exiles and aliens" (1 Pet. 11) in the very Greco-Roman culture they had once called home. Radical hospitality transgresses the boundaries that society holds as sacrosanct. The god of the early Christians was so alien to the pagan world, they were accounted as atheists and soon perse-cuted for it. But the banished host continued to find sanctuary in new human hearts, who kept opening doors to more strangers. The Letter to the Hebrews counsels these expanding networks: "Let mutual love continue. Do not neglect to show hospitality to strangers, for by doing that some have entertained angels without knowing it" (13:1–2).

The early Quaker movement can be compared to the early Christian movement in a number of ways. Radical hospitality is one perspective. The chief conflict of the early movement was against the inhospitality of a state-enforced Church and its enfran-chised clerical class. Similarly to Jesus's reaction to the mercantil-ism of the Jerusalem temple, George Fox recalls in 1649 "when I heard the bell toll to call people together to the steeplehouse, it struck at my life, for it was just like a market-bell to gather people together that the priest might set forth his ware to sale."

By contrast, the Quaker movement was a grassroots phenom-enon gathered through networks of hospitality and mutual aid. The core group of itinerant men and women, "the Valiant Sixty," echoed the seventy sent out by Jesus. The doors that opened to them became places where hospitality exchanged with a free gospel message. Groups met in homes to worship together, to encourage and counsel one another, and to aid families under persecution or other hardship. "Answering that of God in every one" was grounded in the conviction—indeed, the *experience*—that no one is outside the limits of God's love or unable to respond to it. The testimonies that we today codify as simplicity, equality, com-munity, peace, and integrity were forged through the experience of answering that of God in every one. But all of them testified to the living host within and among them. As they befriended the living Christ within, they found friendship extending outward in all directions.

Even through its many changes and revisions over the succeeding 350 years, the practice of hospitality has been constantly renewed among the people called Quakers. The extension of friendship and cooperation in ever-widening circles is the prophetic vocation of the Religious Society of Friends, which takes its rightful place on the outer boundaries of the Christian tradition, the frontiers of the Church. But just as Jesus engaged and never forsook the center of his Jewish faith tradition, Friends must not turn their backs upon the wider Church. Friends too easily make a foil of mainstream Christians, just as Gentile Christians over time made a caricature of Judaism and the Jewish people, with terrible anti-Semitic results. Our witness to the wider Church must remain prophetic and challenging but also collaborative wherever we find common cause in service and social action.

Quaker faith and practice can be compared and combined with a wide variety of other traditions: Buddhism, ethical humanism, and many more. But we will find our deepest and fullest resonances with the biblical Christian traditions that nurtured early Friends and with the Jewish traditions that nurtured Jesus. Friends are present-day pioneers in a stream of radical hospitality that continues to open new doors of friendship and cooperation. Jesus opened that door to us. Let us not banish the host.

ENDNOTES

1 All Bible quotations are from the New Revised Standard Version.

2 See *Quaker Faith & Practice*, Britain Yearly Meeting, 1995, 19.07.

3 Gerald Hewitson's 2013 Swarthmore Lecture, *A Journey into Life: Inheriting the Story of Early Friends*, is an outstanding, articulate example. Available from Woodbrooke Quaker Study Centre at http://www.woodbrooke.org.uk/publications. php?action=publication&id=99.

4 See www.friendsofthelight.co.uk.

5 For a fine Conservative Quaker treatment of Quaker process, see William Taber's *The Mind of Christ* (Pendle Hill Pamphlet #406, Wallingford, PA: Pendle Hill Publications, 2010), edited by Michael Birkel.

6 See "They Too Are Quakers: A Survey of 199 Nontheist Friends" at universalistfriends.org/rush.html.

7 Second edition, New York: O Books, 2005.

8 Pendle Hill Pamphlet #360, Wallingford, PA: Pendle Hill Publications, 2002.

9 *The Quest of the Historical Jesus*, New York: Macmillan, 1968 [1910], p. 403.

10 *The Human Being: Jesus and the Enigma of the Son of Man*, Minneapolis: Augsburg Books, 2001, p. 152.

11 From *Twenty Questions about Jesus* (1985) quoted in *Quaker Faith & Practice*, Britain Yearly Meeting, 1995, 26:33.

DISCUSSION QUESTIONS

1. Who is Jesus to you?

2. What "key orienting experience[s]" in your own life have shaped your perspective on Jesus?

3. As he considers the perspective of foundationist Friends, the author writes, "Any Christian renewal among Friends that draws upon the foundations of our faith and practice will be stillborn if it sits quietly in sectarian rectitude" (p. 15). What do you believe he means by this? What do you see as the crisis of our present time, and who do you believe Christ is, in that crisis?

4. How would you respond to the author's queries to Conservative Friends on p. 16: "What is the heart that beats in the midst of a truly gathered meeting for worship? What is the mind that guides the meeting for business at its best?"

5. How do you tell the story of your own faith to other people?

6. Describe what it means to you, experientially, to "wait upon the Lord," "stand still in the Light," or "sink down to the Seed."

7. How can the Light be both "one with the person of Jesus of Nazareth" and "in all people, in all places and times"?

8. Why does the author affirm the statement of the late Walter Wink, "the raising of Jesus from the dead is an objective fact of history, even if it was not empirically observable"? (See p. 27.) How do you respond to this statement?

9. Who is the Christ you do *not* believe in?

10. How does the author believe Jesus and early Friends exercised "radical hospitality"? How do you believe Friends can express that radical hospitality today?